SURVEY OF THE BIBLE

PART TWO OF THE DEVELOPING GIFTS AND
SKILLS SERIES

DR. HENDRIK J VORSTER

CONTENTS

Survey of the Bible   v

Part I   1

1. Introduction   3
2. The Authority of the Bible   5
3. Making the most of my time in the Word   18
4. Further Study   26

PART II

1. Other Books by Dr Hendrik J Vorster   31

Endnotes   41

SURVEY OF THE BIBLE
PART TWO OF THE DEVELOPING GIFTS AND SKILLS SERIES

-- Disciple Manual --

Survey of the Bible
(Disciple Manual)
Part Two of the Developing Gifts and Skills Series
By Dr. Hendrik J. Vorster

Copyright © 2021 by Hendrik J. Vorster.

All rights reserved. No part of this book may be used or reproduced by any means, graphic, electronic, or mechanical, including photocopying, recording, taping or by any information storage retrieval system without the written permission of the author except in the case of brief quotations embodied in critical articles and reviews.

This book is a work of non-fiction. Unless otherwise noted, the author and the publisher make no explicit guarantees as to the accuracy of the information contained in this book and in some cases, names of people and places have been altered to protect their privacy.

For more copies and information please visit and write to us at: www.churchplantinginstitute.com
resources@churchplantinginstitute.com

Because of the dynamic nature of the Internet, any web addresses or links contained in this book may have changed since publication and may no longer be valid. The views expressed in this work are solely those of the author and do not necessarily reflect the views of the publisher, and the publisher hereby disclaims any responsibility for them.

Scripture quotations marked AMP are taken from the Amplified Bible, Copyright 2015 by the Lockman Foundation. Used by permission.

Scripture quotations marked NIV are taken from e Holy Bible, New International Version, NIV Copyright 1973, 1978, 1984, 2011 by Biblica, Inc. Used by permission. All rights reserved worldwide.

Scripture quotations marked KJV are taken from the King James Version.

ISBN 978-1-955923-14-9

PART I

SURVEY OF THE BIBLE

Part Two of the Developing Gifts and Skills Series

1

INTRODUCTION
SESSION ONE

Jesus taught us *the Spiritual Discipline of having an intake of the Word of God* on a Daily Basis. During His days of Testing, Jesus used the Word to defend and persevere through the temptations Satan tried on Him. Jesus quoted Deuteronomy 8 verse 3 that: *"Man shall not live by bread alone, but by every Word that proceeds from the mouth of God."* On another occasion Jesus presented Himself as the Bread of Life.

Every New Testament Book endorses and encourages us to embrace the Words of the Lord on a daily basis.

Luke 4:4 (NKJV) 4 But Jesus answered him, saying, "It is written, 'Man shall not live by bread alone, but by every word of God.'"

This is what Jesus taught through His example when He faced the Temptation of Satan. Throughout the various aspects of How Satan attempted to seduce and entice Jesus, His defence was consistent: He stood on the Word and used it like a sword and shield.

The Psalmist also tells us of the incredible blessing and impact, meditating and delighting in the Word of God brings.

> *Psalms 1:1-3 NIV "1 Blessed is the one who does not walk in step with the wicked or stand in the way that sinners take or sit in the company of mockers, 2 but whose delight is in the law of the Lord, and who meditates on his Law Day and night. 3 That person is like a tree planted by streams of water, which yields its fruit in season and whose leaf does not wither— whatever they do prospers"*

The Apostle Paul exhorts the church in Colossea to allow the Word of God to dwell richly in them.

> *Colossians 3:16 NIV "16 Let the Word of Christ dwell among you richly as you teach and admonish one another with all wisdom through psalms, hymns, and songs from the Spirit, singing to God with gratitude in your hearts."*

The entrance of the Word of God into our lives, activates the faith we so desperately needs for wholesome and godly living.

> *Romans 10:17 ESV "17 So faith comes from hearing, and hearing through the word of Christ."*

The effectiveness in assimilating and treasuring the Word of God is determined by the heart attitude with which we take time in the Word of God, as well as our willingness and determination to put it into practice.

The Fruitfulness and success of our growth in the Lord, and our Faith in Him, firmly relies on our embracing of the Bible as God's irrevocable Word to us, and the Foundation upon which we will build our Faith and life.

In the following sessions we will briefly explore the Authority of the Word of God, as well as How we may extract the most out of our time in the Word of God. I pray that it will be a huge activator in your life.

2

THE AUTHORITY OF THE BIBLE
SESSION TWO

The Authority of the Bible can be argued from an Archeological, _____, and Prophetic dimension. It is more than coincidence that people without Internet, social media or postal services could speak so accurately into future events, which was fulfilled, unless it was Divinely inspired.

One of the outstanding things Paul taught Timothy was How irrefutable and central the Word of God stands in our lives, and for our well-being.

> *2 Timothy 3:16*
> *All Scripture is God-breathed and is useful for teaching, rebuking,*
> *correcting and training in righteousness,*

The Apostle Peter also emphasised this essential aspect in his Pastoral letter.

> *2 Peter 1:20-21*
> *Above all, you must understand that no prophecy of Scripture came*
> *about by the prophet's own interpretation of things. For*
> *prophecy never had its origin in the human will, but prophets,*

though human, spoke from God as they were carried along by the Holy Spirit.

The Dead Sea _____, amongst other historical manuscripts, support the accuracy of the writings and the inerrancy of the Scriptures. One of the aspects to confirm and validate the Authority of the Scriptures is the _____ of its Message through so many writers, over so many years, from so many varied backgrounds. They all wrote the same consistent message without ever crossing paths to collaborate their perceptions.

Psalm 19:7-9
The law of the Lord is perfect, refreshing the soul. The statutes of the Lord are trustworthy, making wise the simple. The precepts of the Lord are right, giving joy to the heart. The commands of the Lord are radiant, giving light to the eyes. The fear of the Lord is pure, enduring forever. The decrees of the Lord are firm, and all of them are righteous.

They all had the same message and as "their" messages came into fulfillment, their cohesive and divinely ordered origin was affirmed. We often speak about the best Wisdom coming from seeing things in hindsight. The more manuscripts are discovered the more it affirms the miracle of having the "Words of God" in written memory.

We therefor build our lives on the Bible as the inerrant Word of God. I encourage you to hold your Bible in high regard. Treasure its contents as it holds the keys to life eternal. On one occasion Jesus pointed people to the fact that they will remain in error as long as what they do not know the Scriptures.

Matthew 22:29
Jesus replied, "You are in error because you do not know the Scriptures or the power of God."

The Bible is the inerrant Word of God.

The Bible is the most reputable book ever written. The Bible was written over a _____ period by over 40 Authors who wrote Messages from God down as the Holy Spirit inspired them.

- **It can be trusted as the most reliable manuscript ever written**

The many manuscripts confirm its accuracy. *Firstly*, we have the _____ of manuscripts that proof to be exactly the same, and then *secondly*, we have the _____ in the manuscripts, proving beyond doubt their reliability. No other historical document has as many consistent manuscript copies.

- **It consists of a compilation from over 40 writers**

The Authority of the Bible, as the Word of God, is further reinforced by the strong consistent message regardless of being written by over ___ writers, many of whom lived in different time periods and circumstances. The only conclusion can be that the messages were all authored by the Holy Spirit, and reduced to writing by this variety of men and woman. Barely do you find one writer being consistent over his or her own lifetime, yet for these, more than 40 writers, they spoke from one heart and mouth.

- **Written over a 1500-year period**

The period over which these writers wrote spans more than _____ years. To put that in perspective, just think How much life and humanity evolved over the recent 1500 year period, yet, their messages transcended beyond primitivism, class distinctions, education and communicating contextually. The message continues to speak to us regardless of How developed and evolved life might be.

- **More than 5 Billion Bibles printed**

The Bible remains the most printed book of any kind on the planet. No other single book has been reproduced as much as the Bible. This is a remarkable feat since it was outlawed and burned in many riotous revolutions. Many tried to diminish its influence and message throughout its history, yet, regardless of the many attempts to have it destroyed, it remains to be the most printed book year after year.

- **Over 100 million Bibles sold every year**

It is reported, and widely known, that the Bible continues to sell more than a 100 million copies a year.

- **First written book ever printed**

The introduction of the _____ Press also saw the mass production of the Bible as the first book to be reproduced, en-mass in printed form. The Gutenberg Press produced the first ever printed form of any book or manuscripts. It was appropriate that it launched its production lineage with the Bible.

- **Most verifiable and oldest manuscripts of any document on the planet**

It remains one of the remarkable testimonies of the Greatness of God, that God was able to sustain and contain such consistency and meticulous care of each and every manuscript that was ever reproduced of the various writings of the parts of the Bible.

The make-up of the Bible.

The Bible was compiled over a period of time and eventually determined to be the Holy Scriptures as we enjoy it today. The First Canon of Scriptures was the _____ Bible and it consisted of the Old Testament writings as we know it today.

The Hebrew Bible

The Hebrew Bible is historically known as the _____[1], which consist of three parts or compilations.

The **First Part** consist of a compilation of the first five Books of the Bible and was known as the _____.

The **Second compilation** is known as the _____[2] and consist of the *"Former Prophets"*, the books of *Joshua, Judges, Samuel and Kings,* and the Prophetic books of *Isaiah, Jeremiah and Ezekiel and the Twelve Minor Prophets.*

The **third part** consist of the _____[3] which consisted of *Psalms, Proverbs and Job,* then also the *"Hamesh Migillot" which consisted of Lamentations, Esther, Song of Songs, Ruth, Ecclesiastes* and the remaining Books of *Daniel, Ezra-Nehemiah and the Chronicles.*[4]

This three-part compilation became known as the **Tanakh** and was accepted as "Holy Scriptures" by the 2 BC[5]

The Septuagint

The **Septuagint** is the first _____ of the **Tanakh** into **Greek** and is widely used as the standard against which translations are measured. The Septuagint consisted of the Pentateuch, the Historical Books, The Poetic Books and both the Minor and the Major Prophetic Books.

- **The Pentateuch**

The **Pentateuch** consists of the **first** _____ **books** of the Bible. These are the books known to be written by Moses. The Pentateuch consists of *Genesis, Exodus, Leviticus, Numbers and Deuteronomy.*

The Pentateuch gives us a historical account of the first family and how they grew and developed, under the purpose of God into the Israelite family.

The Pentateuch also provides us with a sound biblical framework for godly living through the observance of the laws of Moses, as well as understanding the significance of the Tabernacle as it relates to our daily time with God.

The Pentateuch helps us to understand the Nature of God and His dealing with His people. We learn to know God is the Provider, the Guide, the Great Shepherd, the Miracle Worker, the Deliverer, The Holy God, and the Upper Ruler of the Nations of the World.

The Pentateuch provides us with a solid foundation to build our understanding of God, His Power and Authority. These books will become a constant referencing point in your daily life as it was used and applied in the lives of the Prophets, Jesus, and New Testament Believers.

I pray that your life will be deeply enriched through your journey in the Pentateuch.

- **The Historic Books**

The Historic Books are made up of the all the books that gives us a historic account of the Israelite Nation, their conquest of the Promised Land and how they developed into a Nation operating within Canaan. The Historic Books consists of *Joshua, Judges, Ruth, 1 and 2 Samuel, 1 and 2 Kings, 1 and 2 Chronicles, Ezra, Nehemiah, Esther and Job.*

The Historic Books teaches us on how they won and lost battles as they grew in their faith, as well as bearing the consequences of not walking with God.

The Historic Books give us the Journey of how God led Israel. He first led them through His obedient Servants Moses, Joshua, the Judges, the Priests until they demanded a King.

The Historic Books gives us that account of the Kings and how they led Israel and later the divided Kingdom.

- **The Poetic Books**

The Poetic Books consists of the *Psalms, Proverbs, Ecclesiastes, Lamentations and Song of Songs.*
The Poetic Books provides us with an incredible guidance for godly wisdom and living, as well as great guidance in encapsulating words to express and present our deepest and most earnest thoughts and prayers to God.

- **Prophetic Books**

The Prophetic Books provide us with prophetic utterances which both addressed the people of Israel, Judah as well as Nations and their Leaders through these Prophets.
The Prophetic Books consists of two parts, namely: Major and Minor Prophets. **The Minor Prophets** consists of those Prophets whose personal life and story became a prophetic utterance, as well as God used them to speak to the Kings and people of their time. They are Hosea, Joel, Amos, Obadiah, Jonah, Micah, Nahum, Habakkuk, Zephaniah, Haggai, Zechariah, and Malachi.
The Major Prophets include Isaiah, Jeremiah, Lamentations, Ezekiel, and Daniel. These books were declared "major" because of the amount of text, and not because they were considered more important than the "minor" prophetic books. The Old Testament prophet tended to come into prominence especially during times of crisis. God used the prophets to provide direction and wisdom during times of crisis. They were also used by God to remind the people of their covenantal promises.
The relevance of biblical prophecy is not only the information revealed to the people about the circumstances being faced in their time or in a time to come, but also what the message reveals about the nature of God. Prophecy in the Bible is part of God's self-revelation, by which we come to know God through what he has done in the past and what He plans to do in the future.
Many of these Prophetic Books, not only spoke into their contem-

porary circumstances, but more specifically spoke to future events still to be experienced. Examples of this is found in Daniel, Jeremiah, Isaiah, Joel and Haggai. In fact, almost every one of these Prophets spoke words relevant to the day that we live in.

The Bible

From the Septuagint the Bible was compiled as we have it today. The Septuagint was translated into Greek from the Hebraic text from about 200BC, and then the New Testament Books were written and compiled to make up what is known today as the Bible. This compilation and writing of the New Testament part took until about **100AD**.

The oldest surviving full text of the New Testament is the "**Codex Sinaiticus**", which was "**discovered**" at the St Catherine monastery at the base of Mt Sinai in Egypt in the 1840s and 1850s.[6] Dating from circa 325-360 CE, it is not known where it was scribed, however it is quite possible that it was done in Rome or even Egypt.

Much has been written over the years of various Councils who, under the Guidance of God, determined which letters and Gospels to add to make up the final Canon of Scripture as we know it today. Those books included in the Bible are called canonical, indicating that the group who met together determined that the collection reflect the true representation of God's word and will.

The Bible consists of an **Old Testament** and the **New Testament**. The Old Testament compilations was explored previously.

- **The New Testament**

The New Testament is a collection of 27 books consisting of 4 parts; namely the Four Gospels, the Acts of the Apostles, the Pastoral Epistles and an Apocalyptic Prophetic Book - Revelation.[7] These books were canonized as Sacred Writings and was all written between 50 – 120 AD,[8] and affirmed through the determination at various gatherings of Church Leaders. As early as ____ **AD** at the Council of Rome[9] the incorporation of these 27 books was accepted as part of the complete Bible.

- **Gospels**

The Gospels consists of the Gospel accounts of four of the Apostles namely: ***Matthew, Mark, Luke and John.*** These four books explore the life of Jesus' earthly life and ministry and includes His Teaching to His Disciples. The Gospels also gives us a graphic account of the high prize Christ paid for our redemption. As Believers, we also embrace the instructions given to the Apostles as instructions to us as Believers.

- **The Acts of the Apostles**

The Acts of the Apostles is the account of the Apostle Luke of the ministry and work of the Apostles. It also gives us an insight into the growth and development of the early church. In many ways it is a handbook for those who desire to lead disciple-making churches. It encapsulates the essentials of prayer, witnessing, discipleship, stewardship, study and application of the Word of God and enduring and standing for one's faith in the midst of much persecution.

- **Pastoral Epistles**

The Pastoral Epistles consists of the various letter from Apostles to a variety of churches and individuals with great Christian living teaching and guidance for us today.

- **Revelation.**

The Book of Revelation comprises of a Vision John, the Apostle, had on the Island of Patmos, and prepares us for what lies ahead for the church and the world. It also gives us a correlated outline of things to come in this life and eternity.

Translations of the Bible

The first translation of the Bible, as we know it today, was first available in _____, and then subsequently translated through the years into a number of languages. Nowadays there are many translations, some more closely and accurately translated than others. I recommend a translation that is easier to understand, especially as English is my second language, but also one that will present the truths of God's Words in a responsible and as close as possible to the original way to me.

Through the years I have heard many arguments about the specific translation that should be read. As I contemplated those who more arduously argued on this, I observed very little of the values of the Bible translated in their lives. I believe that we need to embrace God's Word with an openness to hear His voice and a congruent heart attitude to apply and putting it into practice.

I also believe that it is of paramount importance to embrace the Author and what we have in our hands, more than what we lambaste the medium in which His message was brought to us. In the end we have to embrace, whichever translation we use, as the final authority in our lives. SO, whichever translation you use has to bring within you a sense that you believe that this closely resemble the heart and intention of what God wanted to communicate.

The promulgation of Scriptures

- **The Tables of Stone**

The only written instruction God Himself wrote, and gave, was that given to Moses on the Mountain.

Exodus 24:12
The Lord said to Moses, "Come up to me on the mountain and stay

> here, and **I will give you the tablets of stone** with the law and commandments **I have written for their instruction.**"

We have one other account of where the Finger of God wrote a message on the wall in the Book of Daniel. Apart from these two accounts, the rest of the Words of the Lord was reduced to writing under the instruction of the Lord.

- **The writings on Scrolls**

Jeremiah 30:2-3
This is the word that came to Jeremiah from the Lord: "This is what the Lord, the God of Israel, says: 'Write in a book all the words I have spoken to you.'"

I thank God for those obedient Servants of His who wrote down the Words He gave them. It is our responsibility to keep His Words and to ensure that we neither add nor diminish what He said.

- **The Gutenberg Bible**

The 1450 Gutenberg Bible was one of the first known printed books in the world. Printing revolutionized the multiplication of writings. Apart from the origins of the Bible being among the oldest and most reputed among records in the world, the Gutenberg Bible provided the world with the first printed Bible from the original Latin Vulgate. Since its early successes, the Bible continued to be printed and today remains the most sold book in the world year after year.

In Conclusion

During the next session we will explore ways in which we can make the most of our time in the Word.

Assimilation Sheet for
The Authority of the Bible

1. Complete the sentence. *The authority of the Bible can be argued from an Archeological, _____, and Prophetic dimension.*

2. Complete the sentence. *The Dead Sea _____, amongst other historical manuscripts, support the accuracy of the writings and the inerrancy of the Scriptures.*

3. Complete the sentence. *One of the aspects to confirm and validate the Authority of the Scriptures is the _____ of its message through so many writers, over so many years, from such varied backgrounds.*

4. Complete the sentence. *The Bible was written over a _____ period by over 40 Authors who wrote Messages from God down as the Holy Spirit inspired them.*

5. Complete the sentence. *Firstly, we have the _____ of Manuscripts that proof to be exactly the same, and then secondly, we have the _____ in the manuscripts, proving beyond doubt their reliability.*

6. Complete the sentence. *The Authority of the Bible, as the Word of God, is further reinforced by the strong consistent message regardless of being written by over _____ writers, many of whom lived in different time periods and circumstances.*

7. Complete the sentence. *The period over which the writers spans more than _____ years.*

8. Complete the sentence. *The introduction of the _____ Press also saw the mass production of the Bible as the first book to be reproduced, en-mass in printed form.*

9. Complete the sentence. *The first Canon of Scriptures was the _____ Bible and it consisted of the Old Testament writings as we know it today.*

10. What was the Hebrew Bible historically known as? _____.

. . .

11. The Tanakh consisted of three parts. Name the three parts of the Tanakh:

- _____
- _____
- _____

12. What was the first translation of the Hebrew Bible called, and into what language was it translated?
_____
_____

13. The Torah was also known by what name?
_____

14. Complete the sentence. *The Pentateuch consists of the first _____ books of the Bible.*

15. Complete the sentence. *As early as _____ AD at the Council of Rome[10] the incorporation of these 27 books was accepted as part of the complete Bible.*

16. Name the three main ways in which the Word of God was passed down to us in written?

- _____
- _____
- _____
- _____

3

MAKING THE MOST OF MY TIME IN THE WORD
SESSION THREE

How can I make the most of my time in the Word of God? During this session we will explore ways in which we can benefit most from our time in the Word, as well as How this time in the Word can help us grow and mature best.

1. A Good discipline in assimilating the Word of God is to:

- Make a commitment to do it _____.

Nothing impacts our lives as consistently practicing spiritual disciplines. The best way to grow in our faith is by staying connected to the Vine. Sundays are not the only, or best times to have an intake of the Word of God, no, we need a daily intake of the Word.

As much as we know the value of eating daily to nourish and maintain a healthy physical body, we know that a commitment to daily take and receive the Word of the Lord will sustain and maintain a healthy connectedness to the source of all we need.

John 15:7 (NIV)
7 If you remain in me and my words remain in you, ask whatever you wish, and it will be done for you.

- **Set aside a specific and dedicated time to be alone with God and in His _____.**

We usually enjoy breakfast, lunch and dinner around set times. In the same way schedule a time or times in the Word. Set aside a time and place where you can be alone with God and His Word.

- **Find and follow a Bible _____ plan.**

A Reading plan will help you read through the entire Bible on a yearly basis. It also helps us stay on track to consistently have a balanced intake of the Word. Good Bible Reading Plans consist of a portion in the Old Testament, a portion from the New Testament, and often a Psalm or two and perhaps a portion from the Proverbs.

Get a One Year Bible.

These could be found in One-Year Bibles like the Zondervan NIV One-Year Bible. I have seen this being used by my wife for over 30 years. It can be a huge resource and it works!

You could also find Bible Reading Plans on the YouVersion Bible App. The most important thing is that you start one today.

2. The SOAP method

Whilst reading the Bible daily, apply the SOAP method to ensure that you don't just read the Bible as if it is another book, but as it really is: God's Word to you and me to live by.

Make a commitment to put it into practice.

The SOAP method stands for:

- S – _____ (The specific reading of the day),
- O – **Observation** (What is God saying to me through the reading of today?),
- A – _____ (How can I put this into practice today? How can I do this? And make a commitment to do it), and
- P – **Prayer** (Take a few moments to pray the application and commitment into your life.) Eg, *"Heavenly Father, today you spoke to me about forgiveness through Your Word. I choose to forgive like you want me to. I commit to forgive those who are going to do things that I don't like. I forgive them. I forgive those who are harmful and hurtful towards me. Help me to be quick to forgive. Thank you for your forgiveness. Amen"*

3. Listen and do!

Encounter God through your daily reading of the Bible. God speaks, and desires to speak to us as His children. Listen and do! You will always be encouraged and strengthened through the reading and meditation of the Word.

4. Meditate on the Word

Meditate on the Word of God. Pause, while reading, and think about it. Learn the Word of God.

5. Study the Bible.

Take those Scriptures that stand out to you, and those that you sense God is speaking to you about and learn them of by heart, meditate on them and remind God about His promises to you regularly.

6. Be a man and woman of the Word of God.

Where do you start?

A good place to start is to start by reading the Gospel of John. Read at least three chapters of the New and Old Testament a day. Also read 5 Psalms and 1 chapter in Proverbs. This will put you on a good and healthy spiritual discipline diet. It will take you between 15-45 minutes to complete such a regime of reading the Word.

The average reading from a Bible Reading Plans takes about 20 minutes. Combined with meditating and prayer it will require around 60 minutes to give any kind of credence to your effort.

A Good strategy to follow!

You might want to consider the following guidelines when you spend time in the Word:

- **The _____ of the Books**

Each Book has a message. It sometimes helps when you read the Introduction to a Bible Book to ascertain the historical and political background, and contextual time in which the Book was written. It also helps to understand the biblical contemporaries of the time. Many times, there is strong link between some of the Prophets and the time in which a certain Book plays out. This helps to find context as well as build a unified understanding of how God communicates and how our Faithful God works with those who obey and follow Him.

- **God _____ to us through His Word**

Allow the Holy Spirit to speak to you every time you pick up His Word. He wants to speak. Open your heart to hear Him speak to you as you read and contemplate the Word. The Reason He spoke to His people in the Bible is still the same reason He speaks to us today. The very things He addressed with His people in the Bible are still the same things He addresses in us about today.

- **How God spoke to His Servants through the _____**

What often helps is when we make the connection between how God spoke to His Servants throughout the Old Testament, and how He continues to speak to us today. Live with an expectation in your heart that God will speak to you too like He spoke to His Servants throughout the Bible. God spoke in the Old Testament times, Gospel times, and throughout New Testament times.

- **Hear God speak to us _____**

It is essential to know that God speaks to us through the written Word. God also speaks to us through the Holy Spirit while we read and meditate the Word of God. Listen to the Voice of the Holy Spirit. God speaks to us through His Servants who bring the Word of God to us. At some point in your walk with God, God will not only speak to you through His Word, but He will also give you Words to deliver and bring to others. While you read and pray, always keep an openness to understand whether the Lord is speaking to you or wants you to bring encouragement to someone else.

- **It is essential that we _____ by every Word that proceeds from the mouth of God.**

Make a commitment to put the Word into practice. Act on His Word to you, just like the men and woman of God acted and responded to the Words God spoke to them.

- **We need to be _____ by the Word of God.**

In the Old Testament we learn about the Urim and Thummim, the two stones being used to determine outcomes and answers from the Lord.

> Exodus 28:30 (NIV) 30 Also put the Urim and the Thummim in the breastpiece, so they may be over Aaron's heart whenever he enters the presence of the LORD. Thus Aaron will always bear the means of making decisions for the Israelites over his heart before the LORD.

The priest was to establish, beforehand, How the answer of the Lord will be determined. One such occasion was when Saul enquired of the Lord to determine why He never answered him.

> 1 Samuel 14:41-42 (NIV) 41 Then Saul prayed to the LORD, the God of Israel, "Why have you not answered your servant today? If the fault is in me or my son Jonathan, respond with Urim, but if the men of Israel are at fault, respond with Thummim." Jonathan and Saul were taken by lot, and the men were cleared. 42 Saul said, "Cast the lot between me and Jonathan my son." And Jonathan was taken.

We have a number occasions where the Leaders would not proceed before enquiring of the LORD.

> Ezra 2:63 (NIV) 63 The governor ordered them not to eat any of the most sacred food until there was a priest ministering with the Urim and Thummim.

In the same way we need to enquire of the Lord before we make decisions. Let the Word of God guide and direct our footsteps.

Psalms 119:105 (NIV) 105 Your word is a lamp for my feet, and a light on my path.

Proverbs 3:5-6 (NIV) 5 Trust in the LORD with all your heart and lean not on your own understanding; 6 in all your ways submit to him, and he will make your paths straight.

We need to build our lives against the advice gained from the Word of God. Allow God to speak to you on a daily basis, through His Word.

- **Do not _____ or diminish any of the Words of God**

It is essential that we neither read into the Word what it does not say, nor add to what it said. Read and apply it like a child. Take it as it was given to us.

Deuteronomy 4:2 (NIV) Do not add to what I command you and do not subtract from it but keep the commands of the Lord your God that I give you.

Revelation 22:18-19 (NIV) I warn everyone who hears the words of the prophecy of this scroll: If anyone adds anything to them, God will add to that person the plagues described in this scroll. And if anyone takes words away from this scroll of prophecy, God will take away from that person any share in the tree of life and in the Holy City, which are described in this scroll.

In Conclusion

The Word of God is living and active. The Word of God enlightens us by guiding and directing us in the right paths. Every moment we spend in the Word of God, we activate its transformative power to direct us, renew us, strengthen us, guide us and build us up. If His Word remains in us we will bear much fruit.

Assimilation Sheet for
Making the most of my time in the Word

1. Complete the sentence on practicing good disciplines. *Make a commitment to do it_____.*

2. Complete the sentence. *Set aside a specific and dedicated time to be alone with God and His_____.*

3. Complete the sentence. *Find and follow a Bible_____ Plan.*

4. Name the four words in the acronym SOAP.

- S - _____
- O - _____
- A - _____
- P - _____

5. In becoming a Man and woman of the Word there are a few strategies to follow. Complete the following statements.

- *The _____ of the Books*
- *God _____ to us through His Word*
- *How God spoke to His Servants through the _____*
- *Hear God speak to us _____*
- *It is essential that we _____ by every Word that proceeds from the mouth of God*
- *We need to be _____ by the Word of God*
- *Do not _____ or diminish any of the Words of God*

4

FURTHER STUDY

Since most of our disciples may be new to the faith, we need to help them understand, The Bible, its Message, and how to receive and live by it daily. The best way to do this is through an intensive weekend encounter like this one.

To make this Encounter an enhanced experience we recommend that you also complete the "Survey of the Bible" course of Bruce Wilkinson from Teach every Nation. Dr. Bruce Wilkinson is a prolific Teacher and this encounter will enrich your understanding and appreciation of the Word of God.

His "Survey of the Bible" course will help you to:

- See the Big Picture. You'll be introduced to the structure of your Bible so you can manage its content, purposes and applications throughout your life.
- Discover Your Story in *His*. You will see the plan of God in creation and His desire to redeem His people from the consequences of sin and to offer redemption to all of mankind.
- Find Learning Fun. Utilizing memory pegs, animation and

creative staging, difficult content is made mind-easy and memorization become effortless.
- Understand the Historical Timeline. We've broken the historical timeline into 20 different periods – 10 in the Old Testament and 10 in the New Testament.
- Find Out Who, Why and When. You will be able to match 10 key Bible characters with each of those Old and New Testament historical periods.
- Finally, Pinpoint What and Where. You'll explore maps that make sense, to discover where the Garden of Eden was, where Abraham came from, where Jesus walked, Paul was imprisoned and much more.
- Discover Life Change over the Course of Your Lifetime. Consistent review is a crucial element in making this big-picture tool your own. After just a few sessions, you'll be building on this tool for a lifetime of spiritual growth and ministry.

Survey of the Bible Course

You can purchase this material from www.brucewilkinsoncourses.org

PART II

OTHER BOOKS BY DR. HENDRIK J VORSTER

OTHER BOOKS BY DR HENDRIK J VORSTER

Discipleship Foundations - Step One - Salvation Disciple Manual

Step One - Salvation

This Course explores the "How to" be Born Again and to establish a solid Foundation for your faith in Jesus Christ. It is based on Hebrews chapter 6 verses 1 and 2, and explores:

Repentance of dead works,
Faith in God,
Baptisms,
Laying on of hands,
Resurrection of the dead, and
Eternal Judgement

Teacher Manuals and Video Teaching material are available from our website: www.churchplantinginstitute.com

Discipleship Foundations Step Two - Values and Spiritual Disciplines Disciple Manual

Step Two - Values and Spiritual Disciplines Disciple Manual

This Course explores the "How to" develop spiritual disciplines as well as 52 Values Jesus taught. It is based on the teachings of Jesus to His Disciples, and explores:

Spiritual Disciplines

The disciplines we explore are: Reading, meditating on the Word of God, Prayer, Stewardship, Fasting, Servanthood, Simplicity, Worship, and Witnessing.

Values of the Kingdom of God

Humility, Mournfulness, meekness, Spiritual Passion, Mercifulness, Purity, Peacemaker, Patient endurance, Example, Custodian, Reconciliatory, Resoluteness, Loving, Discreetness, Forgiving, Kingdom of God Investor, God-minded, Kingdom of God prioritiser, Introspective, Persistent, Considerate, Conservative, Fruit-bearing, Practitioner, Accountability, Faithful, Childlikeness, Unity, Servanthood, Loyalty, Gratefulness, Stewardship, Obedience, Carefulness, Compassion, Caring, Confidence, Steadfastness, Contentment, Teachable, Deference, Diligence, Trustworthiness, Gentleness, Discernment, Truthfulness, Generous, Kindness, Watchfulness, Perseverance, Honouring and Submissive.

Teacher Manuals and Video Teaching material are available from our website: www.churchplantinginstitute.com

Other Books by Dr Hendrik J Vorster

Discipleship Foundations Step Three - Developing Gifts and Skills

Step Three - Developing Gifts and Skills

This course is run through five weekend encounters. These weekend encounters have been designed to help Disciples discover their spiritual gifts, as well as learn skills to use their gifts, and to serve the Lord for the extension of His Kingdom. The Weekend Encounters are:

Gifts Discovery Weekend Encounter

We learn about Ministerial Office gifts, Service gifts, and Supernatural Spiritual Gifts. We discover our own, and then learn How we may use them to build up the local Church.

Survey of the Bible Weekend Encounter

During this weekend we do a survey of the Bible, from Genesis to Revelation. We also learn about the History of the Bible as well as How we can make most of our time in the Word.

Sharing your Faith Weekend Encounter

During this weekend we learn about the Gospel message, and How to share our faith effectively.

Overcoming Weekend Encounter

During this weekend we deal with those thistles and thorns that smother the growth and harvest of the good seed sown into our lives. We address How to overcome fear, unforgiveness, lust and the cares of the world with faith and obedience.

Shepherd Leader Weekend Encounter

During this weekend encounter we learn about being a Good Shepherd, and How to best disciple in a small group.

Teacher Manuals and Video Teaching material are available from our website: www.churchplantinginstitute.com

34 | SURVEY OF THE BIBLE

Discipleship Foundations Step Four - Fruitfulness

Step Four - Fruitfulness

We were saved to serve. This course has been designed to mobilise Believers from Learners to Practitioners. These sessions have been prepared for individual use with those who are producing fruit.

We explore:

1. Introduction.
2. Walking with purpose.
3. Build purposeful relationships. Finding Worthy Men
4. Priesthood. Praying effectively for those entrusted to you.
5. Caring compassionately.
6. Walking worthily.
7. Walking in the Spirit.
8. Practicing hospitality.

Teacher Manuals and Video Teaching material are available from our website: www.churchplantinginstitute.com

Discipleship Foundations Step Five - Multiplication

Step Five - Multiplication

This course was designed to assist fruit-producing disciples to live a life that will encourage a lifetime of fruitfulness. It will also give disciples skills and guidelines to navigate their disciples through seasons of challenge and growth. We explore:

1. Vision and dreams.
2. Set Godly Goals.
3. Character development
4. Gifts development

Impartation and Activation

5. Fruitfulness comes through constant challenge.
6. Relationships

Family, Children and Friends

7. The Power of encouragement
8. Finances

Personal and Ministry finances

9. Dealing with setbacks

- How to deal with failure?
- How to deal with betrayal?
- How to deal with rejection?
- How to deal with trials?
- How to deal with despondency?

10. Eternal rewards

Teacher Manuals and Video Teaching material are available from our website: www.churchplantinginstitute.com

Values of the Kingdom of God
By Dr. Hendrik J Vorster

Everyone desires to be known as a pleasant to be around with kind of person. This book helps you develop values towards such a godly character. This book explores 52 Values of the Kingdom of God.

Books are available from our website: www.churchplantinginstitute.com

VALUES
OF THE
KINGDOM
OF
GOD

Dr. Hendrik J. Vorster

Spiritual Disciplines of the Kingdom of God
By Dr. Hendrik J Vorster

Every Believer desires to be a Fruit-producing branch in the Vineyard of our Lord. Developing spiritual disciplines is to develop spiritual roots from which our faith can draw sap to grow strong and fruit-bearing branches. This Book explores Nine Spiritual Disciplines of the Kingdom of God.

Books are available from our website: www.churchplantinginstitute.com

SPIRITUAL
DISCIPLINES
OF THE
KINGDOM
OF
GOD

Other Books by Dr Hendrik J Vorster

Church Planting - by Dr Hendrik J Vorster

Church Planting - How to plant a dynamic, disciple-making church
By Dr Hendrik J Vorster

This is a handbook for those who wish to plant a disciple-making church. This book explores every aspect of church planting, and is widely used in over 70 Nations on 6 Continents. Here is a list of the areas that are explored:

1. The challenge to plant New Churches
2. Phases of Church Planting
3. Phase One of Church Planting - The Calling, Vision and Preparation Phase
4. The Call to Church Planting
5. Twelve Characteristics of Church Planting Leaders
6. Church Planting Terminology
7. Phase Two of Church Planting - Discipleship
8. The Process of Discipleship
9. Phase Three of Church Planting - Congregating the Discipleship Groups
10. Understanding Church Planting Finances
11. Understanding Church staff
12. Phase Four of Church Planting - Ministry development and Church Launching Phase
13. Understanding and Implementing Systems
14. Phase Five of Church Planting - Multiplication
15. Understanding the challenges in Church Planting
16. How to succeed in Church Planting
17. How to plant a House Church

Student Manuals and Video Teaching material are available from our website: www.churchplantinginstitute.com

Discipleship Foundation Series on Video

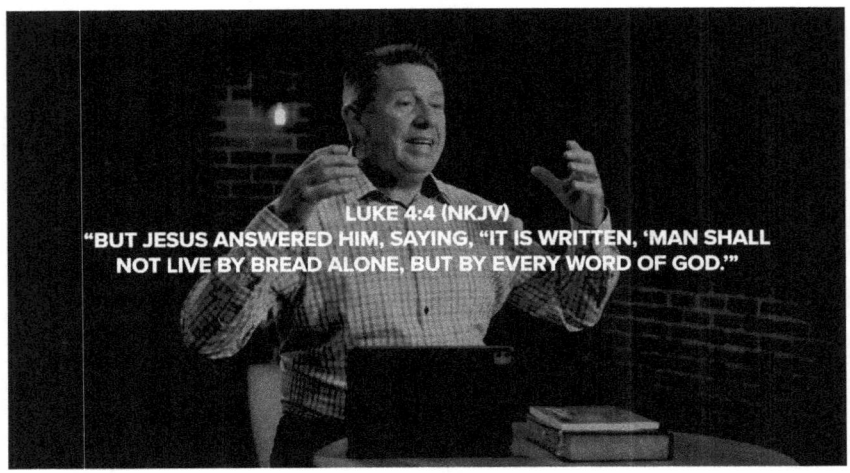

Dr. Vorster teaching via Video

185 Video Teachings are available for each of the Sessions taught throughout these Discipleship Courses.

Discipleship Foundation Series

We have Five, completely recorded, Discipleship Courses available on Video at www.discipleshipcourses.com

- **Step One - Salvation** (*This **7-week course** helps the new Believer to establish, and build a solid Foundation for their faith to build on.*) This course is available, **without charge**, upon free registration.
- **Step Two - Values and Spiritual Disciplines** (*This **9-week** Course helps the young Believer to put down Spiritual Roots, by establishing spiritual disciplines, and by learning the values of the Kingdom of God.*)
- **Step Three - Developing Gifts and Skills** (*This Course is usually presented during **5 Weekend Encounters**, or over a **23-week period**. We explore **Spiritual Gifts** and How to use them*

to build up the local Church. We **explore the Bible**, and its origins, during one part to ensure we build our lives on the Handbook of the Bible. We also learn **How to share our faith**. We learn **How to deal with Strongholds** that might hold us back in fulfilling God's purpose. And finally, we learn **How to best Mentor** those whom we lead to Christ.)
- **Step Four - Discipling Fruit-Producers** (*During this 8-week course* we learn *How to teach our Disciples the principles that will develop, and maintain, fruitfulness.*)
- **Step Five - Multiplication** (*During this 11-week Course* we learn *How to Mentor our Leaders* to lead strong and healthy Fruit-producers.)

Free registration for access to these Video resources is available at www.dicipleshipcourses.com

Church Planting Training Videos

Dr. Vorster teaching via Video

42 Video Teachings are available in this **Church Planting Course.**

- Introduction to Church Planting
- Why plant New Churches?
- Phases of Church Planting Overview
- Phase 1 - Preparation Phase
- Phase 2 - Team Building Phase
- Phase 3 - Prelaunch Phase
- Phase 4 - Launch Phase
- Phase 5 - Multiplication Phase
- Church Planting Trials
- Next Steps

Free Enrolment is available at www.churchplantingcourses.com
Advanced Coaching sessions are available for those who enrolled in the Masters Training Program.

ENDNOTES

2. The Authority of the Bible

1. Miller & Huber, Stephen & Robert (2003). *The Bible: the making and impact on the Bible a history*. England: Lion Hudson. p. 21. ISBN 0-7459-5176-7.
2. https://en.wikipedia.org/wiki/Nevi%27im
3. Neusner, Jacob, The Talmud Law, Theology, Narrative: A Sourcebook. University Press of America, 2005
4. Coogan, Michael D. A Brief Introduction to the Old Testament: the Hebrew Bible in its Context. Oxford University Press. 2009; p. 5
5. Coogan, Michael D. A Brief Introduction to the Old Testament: the Hebrew Bible in its Context. Oxford University Press. 2009; p. 5
6. https://theconversation.com
7. [6] What the Bible is All About Visual Edition by Henrietta C. Mears – Gospel Light Publications, 2007. pp. 438–39
8. Bart D. Ehrman (1997). *The New Testament: A Historical Introduction to the Early Christian Writings*. Oxford University Press. p. 8. ISBN 978-0-19-508481-8.
9. *Saint Justin Martyr*, Encyclopedia Britannica, Inc.
10. *Saint Justin Martyr*, Encyclopedia Britannica, Inc.

www.ingramcontent.com/pod-product-compliance
Lightning Source LLC
Chambersburg PA
CBHW070041070426
42449CB00012BA/3130